Jaromir Jagr

MICHAEL HARLING

GREYSTONE BOOKS

Douglas & McIntyre Publishing Group

Vancouver/Toronto/New York

Greystone Books
A division of Douglas & McIntyre Ltd.
2323 Quebec Street, Suite 201
Vancouver, British Columbia
Canada V5T 4S7
www.greystonebooks.com

Canadian Cataloguing in Publication Data
Harling, Michael, 1958–
    Jaromir Jagr
    (Hockey heroes)

    ISBN 1-55054-836-0

    1. Jagr, Jaromir, 1972– —Juvenile literature.
2. Hockey players—Biography—Juvenile literature.
I. Title. II. Series: Hockey heroes (Vancouver, B.C.)
GV848.5.J35H37 2001   j796.962'092   C00-911470-X

Editing by Lucy Kenward
Cover and text design by Peter Cocking
Front cover photograph by Mitchell Layton
Printed and bound in Hong Kong by C&C Offset Printing Co. Ltd.
Printed on acid-free paper ∞

Every reasonable care has been taken to trace the ownership of copyrighted visual material. Information that will enable the publisher to rectify any reference or credit is welcome.

The publisher gratefully acknowledges the assistance of the Canada Council for the Arts and of the British Columbia Ministry of Tourism, Small Business and Culture. The publisher also acknowledges the financial support of the Government of Canada through the Book Publishing Industry Development Program (BPIDP) for its publishing activities.

Photo credits

Photos on pp. i, iii, iv, 42
by Mitchell Layton

Photos by Bruce Bennett Studios:
pp. 9, 14, 16, 19, 22, 25, 26,
30, 31, 33, 34, 37: Bruce Bennett
pp. 3, 29: John Giamundo
pp. 4, 41: Brian Winkler
pp. 18, 20: Scott Levy

Photos by CTK:
p. 6: Michal Dolezal
p. 10, 13: Stanislav Peska

Photo on page 38
© NHL Images/Dave Sandford

Since joining the NHL

in 1990, Jaromir has

established himself as the

best player in hockey.

CHAPTER ONE

Passing the Torch

On the last day of the National Hockey League's 1998–99 regular season, the eyes of the hockey world were focused on New York. The atmosphere at Madison Square Garden where the Rangers were hosting Jaromir Jagr (pronounced Yar-o-meer Yah-grr) and the Pittsburgh Penguins, was electric. But Jaromir, the league's leading scorer and most valuable player (MVP), wasn't the reason more than 18,200 fans had crowded into the Garden. Nor was he the reason an audience of millions across Canada, the United States, and Europe tuned into the game on television. No, on this Sunday afternoon, hockey fans from Brantford to Brno turned their attention to the Big Apple to see hockey's greatest player ever, Wayne Gretzky, in his last game.

For Pittsburgh, the game was much more than a chance to say goodbye to Gretzky. Unlike the Rangers, who were out of the playoff race, the Penguins were headed for the postseason. But Jaromir and his teammates were not playing well: they had only one win in their last 11 games. A win over New York was important for two reasons. First, the Pens still had a chance to jump to seventh place from eighth in the Eastern Conference. Second, they hoped a win would change their luck going into the playoffs.

The game itself was sloppy and dull. The Rangers spent the afternoon trying to set up Gretzky for one last goal. The Penguins, though, seemed more concerned with not hitting The Great One than winning. Twelve minutes into the second period, however, Pittsburgh opened the scoring. About seven minutes later, Rangers captain Brian Leetch tied the game. Gretzky got an assist, the last point he would record in the National Hockey League (NHL). After three periods, the game was tied, 1–1. The winner would be decided in overtime.

About 70 seconds into the extra period, Pittsburgh defenseman Bobby Dollas stopped a weak

Two of the Greatest

Comparing Jaromir Jagr and Wayne Gretzky is difficult because of their different styles of play. Gretzky, a center, used his crafty playmaking to generate most of his offense. Jaromir relies on his speed and shot to score from the right wing. In the nine seasons they both played in the NHL, though, only Gretzky, with 878 points, had more than Jaromir, who netted 862.

clearing attempt at the New York blueline and slapped the puck into the left corner. Jaromir was tied up by Leetch and couldn't corral the disk as it bounced behind the net. As Jaromir followed the puck into the right corner, Rangers defenseman Mathieu Schneider tried to clear it out along the right boards. But Pens rearguard Greg Andrusak intercepted the puck and shovelled it toward the net.

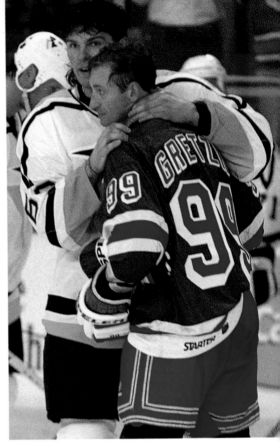

Suddenly, sneaking out of the corner, Jaromir was the only player near the puck. He reached forward for it and was near the bottom of the right faceoff circle, about 15 feet (5 meters) away from the crease, when he took Andrusak's pass on his backhand. Jaromir turned and moved in on goal. He faked New York goalie Mike Richter: forehand, backhand, forehand. Without a prayer, Richter fell to his knees, and Jaromir whipped a wrist shot past the goalie's glove into the net.

In a matter of seconds, the career of the greatest player ever was over. Gretzky, who was on the bench when Jaromir scored, stepped onto the ice. Immediately, a parade of Penguins greeted him, eager to shake his hand. Then Gretzky spotted

Jaromir and skated over to hug him. "I didn't mean to do that," Jaromir apologized, realizing his game-winning goal had spoiled the party. Number 99 understood. "That's what I used to say," he replied.

At the post-game press conference, The Great One was asked about the last goal. Naturally, he was disappointed to lose, but he was quick to praise Jaromir. "Maybe it was fitting," Gretzky declared, "that the best young player in the game scored the goal in overtime. Everyone always talks about passing the torch. He caught it."

For Jaromir, those words were a huge compliment. On a day when the hockey world came to honor Gretzky, The Great One had paid special tribute to Jaromir. After an Olympic gold medal, two Stanley Cups, and three NHL scoring championships, Jaromir was finally recognized as the game's best player. He had come a long way since he left home to join the NHL nine years earlier.

THE JAROMIR JAGR FILE

Position: Right wing

Born: February 15, 1972, Kladno, Czechoslovakia

Height: Six feet two inches (1.88 meters)

Weight: 234 pounds (106 kilograms)

Shoots: Left

Number: 68

Nickname: Jags (Yags)

Hobbies: Drawing, solving brain teasers

Best Friend: Luci, his yellow Labrador retriever

Favorite Foods: Czech wafer cookies, his mother's cooking

Off-Season Sports: Tennis, soccer

Childhood Hockey Hero: Mario Lemieux

Hockey Highlights: Stanley Cup victories, Olympic gold medal

From a frozen pond

near his house to

the city's top pro team,

Jaromir perfected his

game in Kladno.

CHAPTER TWO

The Kid from Kladno

Before Jaromir moved to Pittsburgh to play for the Penguins, he had always lived in Kladno, Czechoslovakia, where he was born on February 15, 1972. Hockey was popular there when he was young, and the city's largest business, the Poldi steelworks, sponsored Kladno's team in the top Czechoslovak League.

When Jaromir was three years old, his father took him skating for the first time, on a frozen pond near their home. As a child, Jaromir's father, whose name is also Jaromir, had hoped to play professional hockey, but a knee injury ended those dreams. Instead, he became an electrician, and when his son was old enough, he encouraged him to play hockey.

The younger Jaromir loved to skate and he was quite good at it, too. During the week, he glided around on the pond, which his father cleared of snow. On weekends, his mother, Anna, took him to Zimni Stadion (Czech for Winter Stadium), the only indoor arena in Kladno. Jaromir was so talented that the figure-skating coaches at the rink tried to sign him up.

When he was four, Jaromir joined a local sports club, Pracovni Zalohy (PZ) Kladno, and started playing hockey. Even though some of the other boys on the team were twice his age, and nearly twice his size, Jaromir was one of the better players because he was a good skater. At practice, the boys would race each other. The whole team would skate one lap of the ice, then on each lap after that, the slowest four players would have to drop out. After the fourth lap, the winner was usually Jaromir.

Jaromir was an All-Star at the 1990 World Juniors.

In Czechoslovakia, teams were made up of boys in the same grade at school. But because Jaromir was such a good player, his father wanted him to skate with older boys. When he was six, Jaromir joined the first-, second- and fourth-grade teams. Playing with the older boys not only gave Jaromir extra ice time, it also meant he had to work hard to keep up. More importantly, though, competing with older boys kept Jaromir from getting cocky. "When I played against other six year olds, I was great. When I played against 10 year olds, I was average," he remembers.

Playing with boys in different grades meant that Jaromir had few close friends off the ice. He should have been pals with boys his own age, but he spent most of his time playing hockey with older boys. Of course, they didn't want to hang out with a little kid, and neither did his only sister, Jitka, who is six years older than he is. So, when Jaromir wasn't playing hockey, he spent a lot of time on his own and became quite shy.

When Jaromir was growing up, a Communist government ruled Czechoslovakia. Often in Communist countries, stores don't stock a lot of goods. Jaromir's parents weren't poor, but they couldn't always buy him things because stores in Czechoslovakia didn't sell them. Most of Jaromir's hockey equipment, for example, was secondhand. But Jaromir knew that hard work, not fancy equipment, makes a player good. When Jaromir started strength training he didn't have weights

to lift, so he used his own body weight instead. Every day he did dozens of knee bends, push-ups, and pull-ups. Later, his father made him some barbells using an old tractor axle. To this day, Jaromir says that the knee bends he did when he was young account for his powerful skating stride.

In the summer, Jaromir played tennis and soccer, two other sports popular in Czechoslovakia. He also gave his father a hand on the family farm. When they went to work on the farm, which was 5 miles (8 kilometers) from their home, Jaromir's father rode his bike and Jaromir followed, running all the way. At the farm, Jaromir helped feed the animals and bring in the hay, a chore that made his arms strong. Jaromir didn't mind pitching in because he knew that working on the farm helped to pay for his new skates. For Jaromir, hockey was never far from his thoughts, even in the summer: every day after the farm work was finished, he took hundreds of shots at a net his father had built in their backyard.

From about the time he was 10, Jaromir and his teammates on PZ Kladno played in national tournaments against the best young teams in Czechoslovakia. Like Jaromir, many of the boys at these competitions, including Jiri Slegr, Martin Straka, and Martin Rucinsky, would later play in the NHL. Against these top players, Jaromir noticed that he wasn't as dominant as he had been when he was younger. He realized that if he wanted to be the best, he would have to work even harder.

Jaromir returns to Kladno each summer to visit his parents.

Occasionally, foreign teams were invited to these tournaments, and Jaromir was able to test himself against the best young talent from around the world. But these international matches also gave Jaromir a chance to trade hockey souvenirs with boys from other countries. Although NHL games were not shown on television in Czechoslovakia, and Jaromir had never watched Wayne Gretzky play, he had heard about him. So, when he got a poster of The Great One, he put it on his bedroom wall. Next to it was a poster of another hero, Martina Navratilova, the Czechoslovak tennis star who lived in the United States.

In 1985, when Jaromir was 13, Prague, the capital city of Czechoslovakia, hosted the World Championships. As Jaromir watched the games, which were shown on national television, he noticed a tall center named Mario Lemieux playing for Team Canada. Lemieux, the NHL Rookie of the Year, thrilled Czechoslovaks when his two goals led Canada to a 3–1 victory over their bitter rivals from the Soviet Union. It was a memorable tournament for Jaromir: Czechoslovakia won the gold medal, and he found a new hockey idol!

Jaromir's professional career began in 1988, about halfway through his second season with the PZ Kladno's top junior team. PZ Kladno didn't have a team in the professional Czechoslovak League but another local club, Poldi Kladno, did. Jaromir had been practicing with Poldi Kladno's pros and, in January, he joined the team for some games in an international tournament in Litvinov, Czechoslovakia. Although he was only 15, and he was paid just 150 Czechoslovak crowns (about $3.50), Jaromir scored in his first game against grown men.

Jaromir often visits young cancer patients in Prague.

During the 1988–89 season, Jaromir played full-time with Poldi Kladno. As a teenager playing against adults, he scored 18 points in 39 games. Just one day after Poldi Kladno's schedule ended, Jaromir joined the Czechoslovak under-18 team

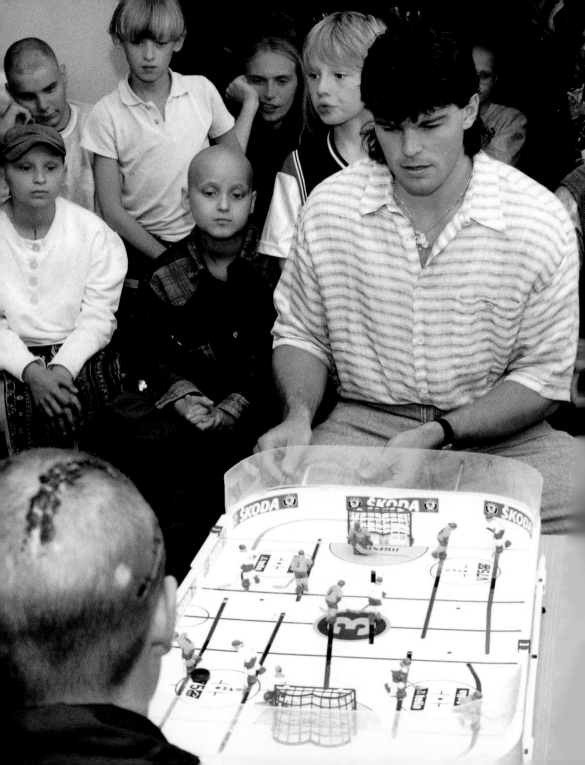

at the European Championships, where the squad won a silver medal. Then, the following September Jaromir played his first game with the men's national team. Czechoslovakia faced off in two games against the Calgary Flames, the 1989 Stanley Cup champions, at an international tournament in Prague. In the second game, Jaromir and his teenaged pals Bobby Holik and Robert Reichel helped their country to a 4–1 victory.

Jaromir led Poldi Kladno in scoring with 30 goals and 59 points in 1989–90. Over the Christmas holidays, he played in the World Junior Championships in Finland. Czechoslovakia won the bronze medal, and Jaromir, who finished second in scoring, was named to the All-Star team. At the end of the season, Jaromir played for the men's national team at the World Championships in Switzerland. In the medal round, Czechoslovakia edged Canada, 3–2. More valuable than the bronze medal he took home, though, was the experience Jaromir gained playing against NHL stars such as Steve Yzerman, Paul Coffey, and Theoren Fleury. When he returned to Kladno, Jaromir knew he was ready for the NHL.

A YOUNG REBEL

The Communist government in Czechoslovakia when Jaromir Jagr was young regarded the United States as its enemy. And Jaromir disliked his own government because it had jailed his grandfathers. So, when he was 12 years old, Jaromir began a small protest against the Communists: he quietly put a picture of Ronald Reagan, the president of the United States, in one of his school books. Had the authorities caught Jaromir, they would have severely punished him. After *Sports Illustrated* first reported this story in 1992, Mr. Reagan telephoned Jaromir to thank him for his support.

In his first two seasons

in the NHL, Jaromir

and the Penguins won a

pair of Stanley Cup

championships.

CHAPTER THREE

Coming to America

Jaromir's hard work began to pay off on October 5, 1990, when he stepped onto the ice for his first NHL game. Although he didn't score, his team, the Pittsburgh Penguins, beat the Washington Capitals, 7–4, at the Capital Center in Landover, Maryland. At first glance, things couldn't have been better for Jaromir: he was 18, earning more money than he could imagine, and playing hockey in the world's best league with his boyhood hero, Mario Lemieux. But for Jaromir, whose future prospects had changed greatly in the past year, the first few months in the NHL were the most difficult of his life.

Less than a year before his NHL debut, playing in North America had been an impossible dream for Jaromir. The Communist government in Czechoslovakia did not allow star athletes to live and play in other countries. Those who did leave the country, like tennis player Martina Navratilova, could never return for visits. For Jaromir, who is very close to his family, leaving forever (called "defecting") was not a choice. Fortunately, things changed during his last season in Kladno.

In November 1989, a group of university students hoping for freedom protested against the government in Prague.

These rallies were very dangerous: in 1968, Communists from the Soviet Union invaded Czechoslovakia to crush another freedom movement. But in 1989, times were different. People all over Czechoslovakia joined the protests. Even some hockey games were cancelled when the players went to the demonstrations. By the end of the month, Czechoslovakia had a new, democratic government.

The new government allowed athletes both to leave the country and to come back, so after the Penguins picked Jaromir fifth overall in the 1990 Entry Draft, he was able to play in the NHL. Because he didn't speak any English, Jaromir moved to

Pittsburgh two months before the season started so that he could go to school. To help him adjust to the American way of life, he lived with a Czech family in Pittsburgh.

Jaromir played well at training camp and looked good as he started his rookie season. He scored his first NHL goal in his second game, a 7–4 win over the New Jersey Devils at the Civic Arena in Pittsburgh. But soon after, his play began to slip. He was having trouble adapting, not only to the faster NHL game, but also to his new life in a strange land. Once again, Jaromir was the youngest player on the team. He was shy and didn't speak English, and so he had trouble making friends. Even worse, he couldn't understand what Penguins coach Bob Johnson wanted him to do on the ice. Often, Jaromir tried too hard to make a good play and he would make a mistake instead.

In November, he began a 15-game slump during which he scored no goals and only one assist. After one of these games Jaromir started crying in the dressing room. His NHL dream had turned into a nightmare: he was homesick, he had no friends, and his play was lousy. Jaromir began to doubt that he was good enough to play in the NHL, and he thought about going home to Kladno.

Then, on December 13, Jaromir received an early Christmas present when the Penguins acquired Jiri Hrdina in a trade with the Calgary

It's Raining Pucks

In February 1992, Jaromir Jagr got a 10-game suspension for bumping a referee during an argument. While he was suspended, Jaromir practiced his English by reading the weather at WDVE-FM, a Pittsburgh rock 'n' roll radio station. But not all his forecasts were clear. "It's always 'partly cloudy,'" teammate Rick Tocchet joked, "because that's all he knows how to say."

Flames. At last, someone else on the team spoke Czech. Hrdina, a star in Czechoslovakia before joining Calgary three seasons earlier, helped Jaromir on the ice and became his friend away from it. "The first three months didn't go very well and I got frustrated and I wanted to go home," Jaromir said later of his early days with the Penguins. "After that they traded for Jiri and my game turned around." Playing on a line with Hrdina and Bryan Trottier, Jaromir's confidence returned. He began scoring again, notching 37 of his 57 points in the final 40 games of the season.

Jaromir's solid performance spilled over into the playoffs. In the second game of the opening series against New Jersey, he made a great individual play to score the winning goal in over-time. Although Jaromir tallied three goals and 10 assists, it was the veterans, such as Mark Recchi, Kevin Stevens, and especially Mario Lemieux, who carried the team through the postseason against Washington, Boston, and Minnesota. And on May 25, it was Lemieux, the Penguins captain and the MVP in the playoffs, who hoisted the Stanley Cup in victory.

THE PRAGUE SPRING

In the spring of 1968, Alexandr Dubcek, the leader of the Communist Party of Czechoslovakia, gave his citizens some new freedoms. Soon, Czechoslovaks, especially in Prague, were happily listening to rock 'n' roll music and watching American movies. But not all Communists liked the changes. In August 1968, the Soviet Union, the most powerful Communist nation, invaded Czechoslovakia and ended what was called communism "with a human face." Jaromir Jagr wears number 68 on his hockey jersey to honor those who fought for Czechoslovakia's freedom during the Prague Spring.

Jaromir felt much more comfortable in Pittsburgh during his second season, when he scored 69 points in 70 games. To help him improve his English, he lived with an American family. He also bought a car so that he no longer had to rely on George Kirk, a Penguins employee, to drive him everywhere. In January 1992, Jaromir played in the NHL All-Star game. But it was in the playoffs that he shone the brightest.

In the seventh game of the opening round against Washington, Jaromir scored to win the game and the series. Then, in Game 2 of the next round, New York Rangers forward Adam Graves broke Lemieux's left hand with a vicious slash. With their captain sidelined, the Pens needed someone to lead the team. That someone was Jaromir: in the five games Lemieux missed, Jaromir scored three game-winning goals.

A bump on the road to the 1991 Stanley Cup.

Later, in Game 1 of the finals against Chicago, Jaromir deked around three Blackhawks and scored a brilliant third-period goal to tie the game. "It's probably the greatest goal I've ever seen," exclaimed Lemieux, who netted the winner five minutes later. "Play hard, and good things happen," Jaromir said of his goal. Six days later, the hard-playing Penguins captured their second Stanley Cup in as many years. This time, though, Jaromir had played a much bigger role. Having worked through some tough times early in his career, Jaromir was now starting to show signs of becoming a great player.

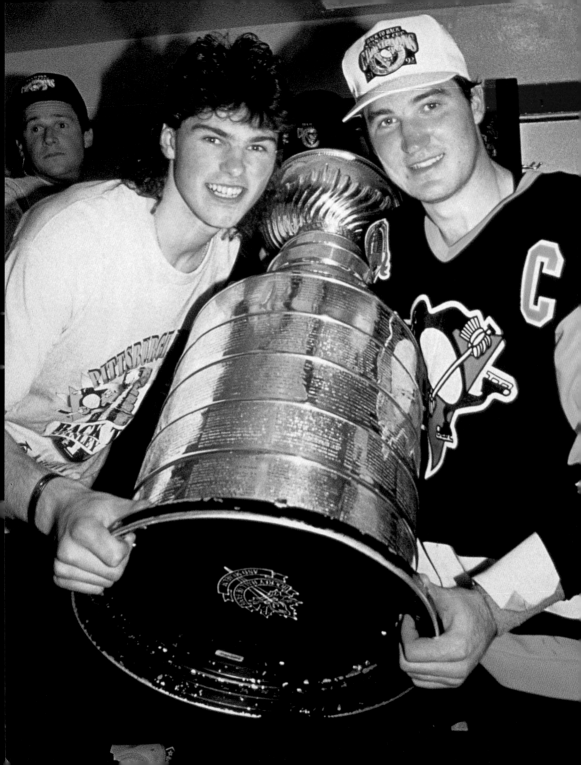

After back-to-back

Stanley Cups, Jaromir

and the Penguins hoped

to build a dynasty.

CHAPTER FOUR

The Secret of Success

Two seasons, two Stanley Cups.
For Jaromir, winning champion-
ships was becoming a habit. Heading into the 1992–93 season,
there was little reason to doubt that Pittsburgh couldn't win its
third straight title. The back problems that had bothered
Lemieux during the last few years seemed to be behind him.
And, after his playoff performance, Jaromir was confident he
belonged in the NHL.

In the regular season, the Pens did as expected, finishing
first in the league. Jaromir chipped in with 94 points, his best

total yet. But unlike the year before, he couldn't raise his play when the team needed it most. In January, doctors discovered that Lemieux had a type of cancer called Hodgkin's disease. While he received radiation treatments, Lemieux was out of the lineup for about seven weeks. In the 19 games Jaromir played while Lemieux was on the disabled list, he managed only five goals, none of them game winners.

In the first round of the playoffs, with Lemieux back on the ice, Pittsburgh took care of the New Jersey Devils in five games. The next series was against the New York Islanders, a team that finished the regular season with 16 fewer wins than the Penguins. Lemieux's bad back returned, though, and he struggled to play in the seven-game series. Jaromir scored three times against the Islanders, including the winner in Game 3. But in the final two contests, both of which Pittsburgh lost, Jaromir was shut out. Once again, he was unable to step up his play.

Jaromir was having trouble adjusting to his role as one of the Penguins' best players. When Lemieux, still Pittsburgh's leading player, was in the lineup, the other teams sent their top

REACH FOR THE TOP

During his first 10 seasons in the NHL, Jaromir Jagr notched 958 regular-season points, placing him third in all-time scoring by Czechoslovak-born players. If he stays healthy and keeps producing at his current pace, Jaromir should pass the leader, Stan Mikita, sometime in 2005. Mikita, who col- lected 1467 points in 22 seasons with the Chicago Blackhawks, was born in Slovakia but he moved to Canada as a boy. Although Mikita was the league's top sniper four times in the mid-1960s, Jaromir is the first Czechoslovak-trained shooter to win the NHL scoring title.

checkers out against him. So, Jaromir had more room to play when he was on the ice, but since Lemieux was on the first line, Jaromir and the second line didn't get as much playing time. With Lemieux out of the action, Jaromir got more ice time, but the other teams knew he was a scoring threat and shadowed him closely. Just like when he first played in national tournaments as a boy, Jaromir knew he would have to work harder to become the best player in the NHL.

Fittingly, playing for Poldi Kladno in 1994 taught Jaromir to pick up his game. That fall, NHL team owners and the players had a disagreement over money. During the dispute, which lasted until January, no games were scheduled, so Jaromir went home to play in the Czech Republic. (In 1993, Czechoslovakia became two countries, the Czech Republic and Slovakia.) Although he was earning almost $4 million per season in the NHL, when Jaromir suited up for Poldi Kladno he played for free.

Hockey fans in the Czech Republic were eager to see Jaromir compete in his first games in the Czech Extraleague since becoming an NHL star. And as the top hockey player ever from the Czech Republic, Jaromir put a lot of pressure on himself to perform well for his Czech fans. But when he arrived in Kladno near the end of October, Jaromir had been off the ice for almost a month. He was out of shape. "I sat around like a couch potato and gained weight," he remembers. So, Jaromir had to dig down deep and find that something extra he needed for his top game. Driven only by the desire to be the best, Jaromir played through the pain of some minor injuries to help the team. In 11 games, he tallied eight goals and 22 points. More important, though, was the team's success: Poldi Kladno jumped from ninth place to second while Jaromir was in action.

Back in the NHL after the dispute was settled, Jaromir put his newfound drive to good use. Because of his continuing health problems, Lemieux sat out the entire season. This time, though, Jaromir stepped forward during Lemieux's absence. After 13 games, he led the league in scoring with 28 points. In the final game of the shortened season, he scored his 70th point to capture the league scoring title. He was the first player other than Lemieux or Gretzky to lead the league in scoring since 1980. Jaromir also came in second in the voting for the NHL's most valuable player. The Penguins did well too, placing third overall in the league. And even though the New Jersey Devils, the team that would later win the Stanley Cup, knocked Pittsburgh out in the second round of the playoffs, Jaromir had proven he could be one of the best.

Momma's Boy

Not many NHL superstars live with their mothers, but Jaromir Jagr does. During his first two seasons, Jaromir's mother, Anna, visited him often. But since then, she's lived with him in Pittsburgh during the hockey season. One of the most important things she does for Jaromir is cook. She also helps him answer some of the thousands of fan letters he receives every year.

Jaromir's powerful

legs allow him to

accelerate with the puck

through open ice.

CHAPTER FIVE

Greatest in the Game

Jaromir's new, determined approach toward every game proved even more successful in 1995–96. With a roster that included Jaromir, Ron Francis, and a healthy Lemieux, Pittsburgh led all NHL teams in scoring and finished fourth in the regular-season standings. Jaromir posted his best numbers to date. His 87 assists and 149 points were NHL records for a right winger and placed him second to Lemieux in the scoring derby. Unfortunately for the Penguins, their season ended early when the Florida Panthers eliminated them in Round 3 of the postseason.

Jaromir's play was excellent for two main reasons. First, his 1995 scoring title gave him confidence. "For the first time he understood he was one of the top players in the league," Penguins coach Eddie Johnston observed during the 1996 playoffs. Second, Jaromir began making full use of his abilities. Some of these qualities, such as his size and his incredibly long reach, he was born with. The way he uses these natural gifts, though, is what sets him apart, according to former Penguins coach Scotty Bowman. "A lot of big guys play with their sticks tight to their bodies and don't use that reach to their advantage like Jaromir does."

Many of his other talents, including his strength and skating, result from Jaromir's dedicated training as a boy. "He's a gorilla, strong as a horse," noted Johnston. "I don't know anybody who's stronger on his skates." Indeed, Jaromir's strength gives him a big edge in traffic near the opposing team's net. His powerful legs make it difficult for defenders to knock him off the puck and, combined with his magical stickhandling, it's almost impossible for opponents to strip the puck off his stick.

Jaromir helped the Czechs win the 1998 Olympic gold medal.

Jaromir's conditioning, which was inspired by his former Penguins teammate, superstar defenseman Paul Coffey, allows him to log more ice time than most forwards. "I looked at Paul and he was riding the exercise bike," Jaromir remembers. "That's when I started to do it. He made me realize that working hard during practice and riding the bike, even the good players do that."

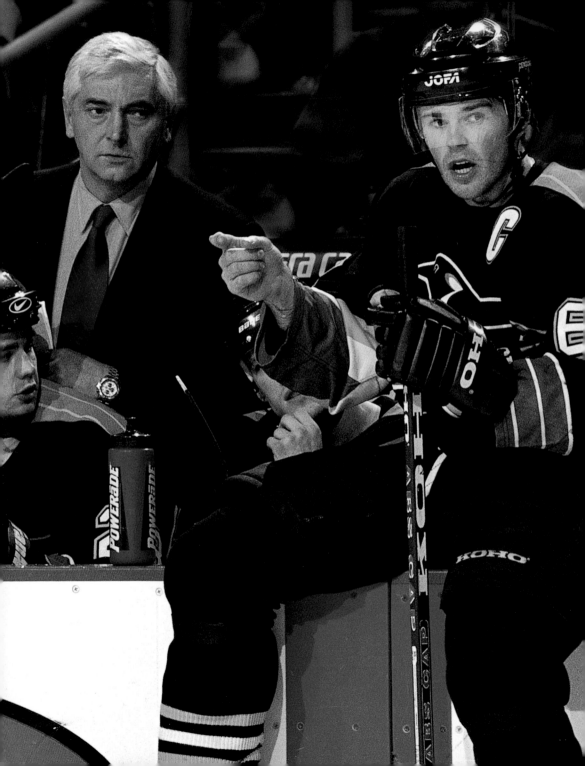

The 1997–98 season marked the beginning of a new era for the Pittsburgh Penguins. Mario the Magnificent, the player Jaromir idolized as a teen and patterned himself after as a pro, had retired. "Every student needs a teacher," Jaromir recalled, "and he was my teacher." The team's new captain was Ron Francis, the center on Jaromir's line. With Francis feeding him the puck, Jaromir captured his second NHL scoring title. The Penguins finished fourth in the regular season but were upset by the Montreal Canadiens in the opening round of the playoffs.

The highlight of Jaromir's year, though, was the 1998 Winter Olympics in Nagano, Japan. The Czech Republic, with only 11 NHL players, was not expected to do well against the teams from Canada and the United States, which were completely made up of NHLers. But Czech coach Ivan Hlinka's squad played disciplined defensive hockey. Thanks to the spectacular goaltending of Dominik Hasek, the Czechs edged their archrivals from Russia to win their first-ever gold medal in Olympic hockey. For the Czech people, this victory was the most exciting event since they overthrew the Communists in 1989.

CZECH MATES

In 1990, when Jaromir Jagr joined the Penguins, he was the only Czech on the team. Ten years later, he had lots of company: on the opening day of the 2000–01 season, nine other Czechs found a place on Pittsburgh's 24-man roster. Ivan Hlinka, the coach of the Penguins, is Czech, too. The team also included seven Canadians, two Americans, two Russians, a Swede, a Finn, and a Lithuanian. Fitting for this multinational squad, the Penguins began their season with a pair of games against the Nashville Predators in Tokyo, Japan.

At the start of the 1998–99 season, the Penguins had money problems. Things were so bad that the Pens let Francis sign with another team, the Carolina Hurricanes. Jaromir became Pittsburgh's new captain, an unfamiliar role. "I never had a chance to know what it was to be a leader," Jaromir said of his years playing with Lemieux. "I was always the youngest, the baby." Once again, Jaromir led the league in scoring, but in the postseason the Pens couldn't get past a second-round tilt with the Toronto Maple Leafs.

Two months after their last on-ice meeting at Madison Square Garden, Jaromir and Wayne Gretzky met again. This time the scene was the NHL awards ceremony in Toronto. Gretzky was presenting the Hart Trophy, which he won a record nine times, to the league's MVP, Jaromir Jagr. When he was growing up in Kladno, Jaromir dreamed of being the best: now he was. "It's even more special," the excited Czech said, "because Wayne Gretzky is standing behind me right now."

Jaromir is always the focus of opposing checkers.

When the league's MVP, Jaromir, showed up at training camp in September 1999, he caused quite a stir. During the summer, Jaromir had visited a barber and had his famous locks shortened. The haircut was a sign that Jaromir had grown up and was taking his job as captain seriously. The new 'do wasn't the only change in Pittsburgh that season, though. Two years after he hung up his skates, Mario Lemieux returned to become the Penguins' new owner, saving the team from going out of

business. And Jaromir won the league's scoring crown for the third year in a row, a hat trick that his new boss never managed.

In December 2000, the hockey world was surprised by news that Super Mario was coming out of retirement to play again for the Penguins. Just 33 seconds into Lemieux's first game in 3½ years, Jaromir jammed a pass from Number 66 behind Toronto goalie Curtis Joseph. By the end of the season, Jaromir had tallied 121 points, enough to win his fifth scoring title. But after Pittsburgh lost in the third round of the playoffs, Jaromir asked to be traded. "To be on the team, I didn't think it would be good for me or good for Pittsburgh," he explained later.

On July 11, 2001, the Penguins sent Jaromir to their Eastern Conference rivals, the Washington Capitals. With Jaromir, and stars such as Peter Bondra and Olaf Kolzig, the Caps should be one of the NHL's top squads. At the press conference introducing him as a Capital, Jaromir was very excited about the possibility of bringing Washington its first championship. "We have a good team, a great team," he said. "To win the Stanley Cup, you have to be very lucky. Hopefully we can do it." Jaromir, though, is too much of a professional to depend on luck. He'll meet the challenge of winning another Stanley Cup the way he's met other challenges in his life—with determination and hard work.

Old Friends

On October 5, 1990, when the Pittsburgh Penguins met the Washington Capitals, two future stars, Jaromir Jagr and Peter Bondra, made their NHL debuts. Since the beginning of the 1994–95 season, Jaromir (314) and Peter (281) have been the NHL's top goal scorers. Although the two wingers grew up in Czechoslovakia, they never played together until Jaromir was traded.

STATISTICS

Czechoslovak/Czech Leagues

Year	Team	GP	G	A	P	PIM
1984–85	Poldi Kladno-B	34	24	17	41	–
1985–86	Poldi Kladno-B	36	41	29	70	–
1986–87	Poldi Kladno-Jr	30	35	35	70	–
1987–88	Poldi Kladno-Jr	35	57	27	84	–
1988–89	Poldi Kladno	39	8	10	18	4
1989–90	Poldi Kladno	51	30	29	59	–
1994–95	Poldi Kladno	11	8	14	22	10
Totals		236	203	161	364	14

International Hockey

Year	Event	GP	G	A	P	PIM
1990	World Juniors	7	5	13	18	6
1990	World Championships	10	3	2	5	2
1992	Canada Cup	5	1	0	1	0
1994	World Championships	3	0	2	2	2
1997	World Cup	3	1	0	1	2
1998	Olympics	6	1	4	5	2
Totals		34	11	21	32	14

Key

GP = Games Played   G = Goals   A = Assists

P = Points   PIM = Penalties in Minutes

National Hockey League (NHL)

Regular Season

Year	Team	GP	G	A	P	PIM
1990–91	Pittsburgh	80	27	30	57	42
1991–92	Pittsburgh	70	32	37	69	34
1992–93	Pittsburgh	81	34	60	94	61
1993–94	Pittsburgh	80	32	67	99	61
1994–95	Pittsburgh	48	32	38	70	37
1995–96	Pittsburgh	82	62	87	149	96
1996–97	Pittsburgh	63	47	48	95	40
1997–98	Pittsburgh	77	35	67	102	64
1998–99	Pittsburgh	81	44	83	127	66
1999–00	Pittsburgh	63	42	54	96	50
2000–01	Pittsburgh	81	52	69	121	42
Totals		806	439	640	1079	593

Playoffs

Year	Team	GP	G	A	P	PIM
1991	Pittsburgh	24	3	10	13	6
1992	Pittsburgh	21	11	13	24	6
1993	Pittsburgh	12	5	4	9	23
1994	Pittsburgh	6	2	4	6	16
1995	Pittsburgh	12	10	5	15	6
1996	Pittsburgh	18	11	12	23	18
1997	Pittsburgh	5	4	4	8	4
1998	Pittsburgh	6	4	5	9	2
1999	Pittsburgh	9	5	7	12	16
2000	Pittsburgh	11	8	8	16	6
2001	Pittsburgh	16	2	10	12	18
Totals		140	65	82	147	121